HOW TO WIN
IN THE RING

Written by Steve Pantaleo

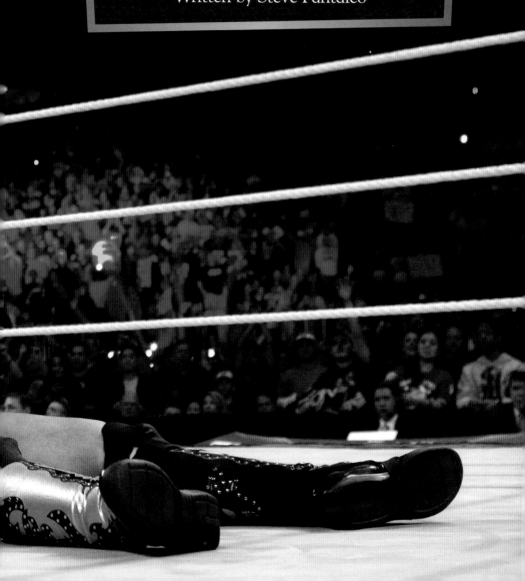

HOW TO WIN
IN THE RING

Written by Steve Pantaleo

For DK
Senior Editor Tori Kosara
Editors Pamela Afram, Rosie Peet
Editorial Assistant Vicky Armstrong
Senior Designers Nathan Martin, David McDonald, Mark Penfound
Designers Sunita Gahir, Lisa Sodeau
Cover Designer James McKeag
Pre-Production Producer Kavita Varma
Producer Zuzana Cimalova
Project Manager Clare Millar
Managing Editors Sarah Harland, Paula Regan
Managing Art Editors Jo Connor, Vicky Short
Publisher Julie Ferris
Art Director Lisa Lanzarini
Publishing Director Simon Beecroft

Reading Consultant Linda B. Gambrell, Ph.D

For WWE
Global Publishing Manager Steve Pantaleo
Photo Department Lea Girard, Melissa Halladay, Mike Moran,
Jamie Nelson, JD Sestito, Josh Tottenham, Frank Vitucci
Legal Lauren Dienes-Middlen

First American Edition, 2019
Published in the United States by DK Publishing
1450 Broadway, Suite 801, New York, NY 10018
DK, a Division of Penguin Random House LLC

Contains content previously published in:
DK Reader Level 2 WWE *How To Be A WWE Superstar* (2017),
DK Reader Level 2 WWE *Tag Teams and Team-Ups* (2019)

Page design copyright © 2019 Dorling Kindersley Limited

19 20 21 22 23 10 9 8 7 6 5 4 3 2 1
001–316426–Dec/2019

A catalog record for this book is available from the Library of Congress.

ISBN 978-1-4654-9048-3 (Hardback)
ISBN 978-1-4654-9038-4 (Paperback)

DK books are available at special discounts when purchased in bulk for sales promotions,
premiums, fund-raising, or educational use. For details, contact: DK Publishing Special Markets,
1450 Broadway, Suite 801, New York, NY 10018
SpecialSales@dk.com

Printed and bound in China

www.wwe.com
www.dk.com

A WORLD OF IDEAS:
SEE ALL THERE IS TO KNOW

Contents

6   How to be a WWE Superstar

48   Tag Teams

72   Team-Ups

90   Quiz

94   Glossary

HOW TO BE A WWE
SUPERSTAR

Written by Steve Pantaleo

Welcome to WWE!

WWE Superstars are some of the toughest athletes on the planet.

Finn Bálor

Roman Reigns

More than 100 Superstars compete each week on *RAW* and *SmackDown Live*. Only the best competitors win big prizes called championships.

What makes a WWE Superstar?

No two WWE Superstars are alike. Some rely on strength to win a match. Others use moves that surprise their foes. Look at Seth Rollins fly!

A big personality is also important. Sasha Banks likes to make the crowd cheer. Her nickname is The Boss.

Getting ready

Superstars are always preparing for the next match. They aim to work harder than their rivals. Dolph Ziggler trains every day. He lifts weights and does box jumps to stay strong.

WWE Performance Center

New competitors train at WWE's Performance Center. They learn the skills they need to become WWE Superstars.

There are seven practice rings inside the Performance Center. WWE athletes exercise and practice their moves here.

Match ready

Superstars battle in several types of matches. In a Ladder Match, Superstars must reach the top and be the first to grab a hanging object. At 20 feet high, WWE's ladders are taller than a giraffe!

In a Steel Cage Match, competitors battle inside a giant cage. The tall sides of the cage make it difficult for Superstars to get in or out.

Making an entrance

Superstars arrive for matches in style. The Rock excited the crowd at *WrestleMania* 32 with a fiery entrance.

Cheering crowds

Superstars love to get the crowd roaring. They come up with fun ways to get cheers, or even boos!

The New Day are always popular with the crowd. They wear bright outfits. Xavier Woods plays a trombone to excite the audience.

Signature moves

Some Superstars use special
moves to help them win a match.
These are called signature moves.

Becky Lynch tugs on her
opponent's arm to make her give
up. Neville performs his Red
Arrow move. He twists in midair
and crashes down on a fallen foe.

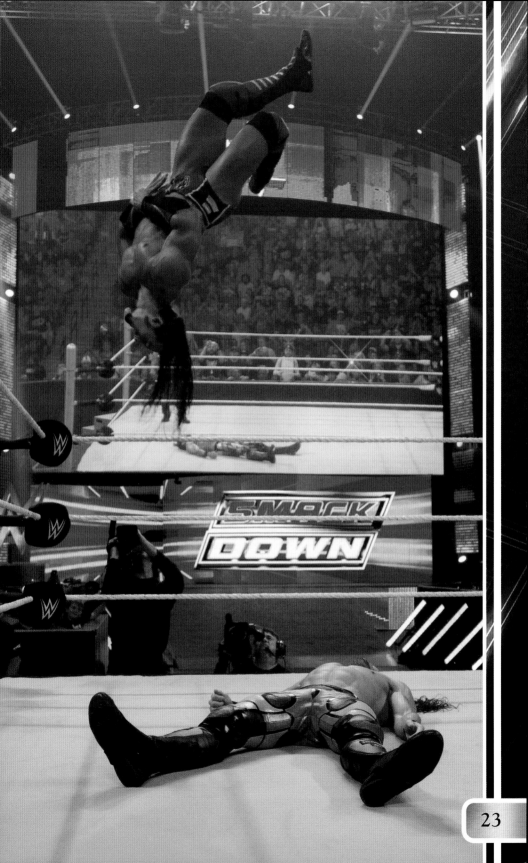

Finishing moves

Many Superstars use special moves to help them end a match and win it.

F-5

Brock Lesnar twists like a powerful tornado to throw opponents off his shoulders.

RKO

Randy Orton pulls opponents to the mat with force.

SHARPSHOOTER

Natalya uses this move to make opponents give up. Her uncle, Bret "Hit Man" Hart, made this move famous.

Role of a manager

Managers give Superstars advice before and during a match. They tell Superstars what to do in the ring to win.

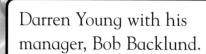

Darren Young with his manager, Bob Backlund.

Manager Maryse does not agree with the referee's decision. She wants him to change his mind so that The Miz can win.

Rules of the ring

WWE referees make sure Superstars follow the rules. A competitor can be disqualified if they try to cheat.

There are a lot of rules to follow. For example, Superstars cannot touch a referee. They are also not allowed to leave the ring for more than 10 seconds.

However, some Superstars try to distract the referee so that they can win by cheating when the referee isn't looking.

The referee reminds Jack Swagger to obey the rules or he will be disqualified!

Bending the rules

Some WWE Superstars do not follow any of the rules. Here are some sneaky moves to watch out for!

SNEAK ATTACK

Superstars sometimes surprise their opponent with a sneak attack as they enter the ring.

HIDDEN OBJECT

Some competitors try to hide an object in their outfit to use in the match.

PULLING TIGHTS

A Superstar might try to pin an opponent by pulling on their tights. This is not allowed!

Alexa Bliss surprises her rival, Becky Lynch, from behind.

Facing rivals

Many Superstars have a rival.
A rival is someone they are always
trying to beat. John Cena and
Randy Orton both became
Superstars in 2002. They have
been rivals ever since.

John Cena tries his best to win in every match. He knows Randy will try his hardest, too.

Know your rivals

A WWE Superstar must know who their enemies are. Then they will know how to beat them.

NAME:
Dean Ambrose

LIKES:
Danger

DISLIKES:
Wearing tights

WATCH OUT FOR:
Unexpected moves

NAME:
John Cena

LIKES:
Hard work

DISLIKES:
Taking shortcuts

WATCH OUT FOR:
Determination. John Cena never gives up.

NAME:
Charlotte Flair

LIKES:
Her WWE family history

DISLIKES:
Not getting what she wants

WATCH OUT FOR:
Sneak attacks from her friends

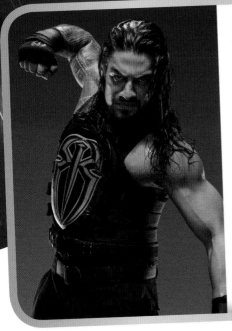

NAME:
Roman Reigns

LIKES:
People who say he can't do something. He will prove them wrong!

DISLIKES:
Big mouths

WATCH OUT FOR:
His powerful Superman Punch

Tag team power

Two or more Superstars can join
forces and become a tag team.
The Usos are twin brothers.
They have always been a team.

Sheamus and Cesaro did not like each other when they teamed up. The two Superstars soon learned to work together.

Terrific tournaments

A tournament is made up of many matches. To win the tournament, Superstars must win every match.

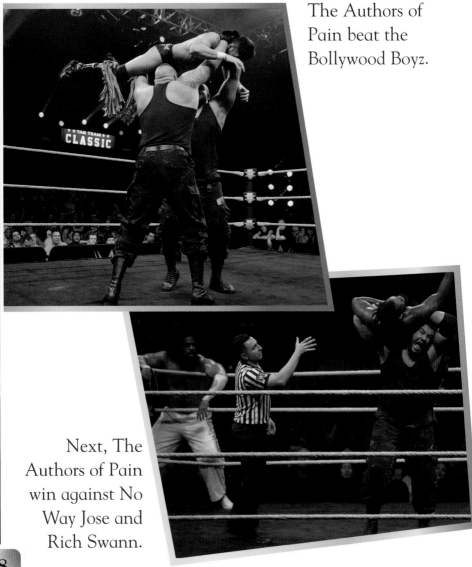

The Authors of Pain beat the Bollywood Boyz.

Next, The Authors of Pain win against No Way Jose and Rich Swann.

The Authors of Pain
win the tournament.

Superstars must be ready for any
opponent. It is hard to stay strong
during so many matches. Finally,
the winners get a shiny trophy!

Championships

Every Superstar wants to win a
championship. They are the biggest
prizes in WWE. Superstars work
very hard to win them.

Dolph Ziggler
wins the
Intercontinental
Championship.

Winning a championship makes a Superstar's hard work worth it. The champions love to cheer and celebrate!

Rhyno and Heath Slater win the *SmackDown* Tag Team Championship.

Becky Lynch wins the *SmackDown* Women's Championship.

Legendary champions

Some Superstars have won a championship more than once.

NAME:

Shawn Michaels

TITLE:

WWE Championship

NUMBER OF TIMES WON:

Three

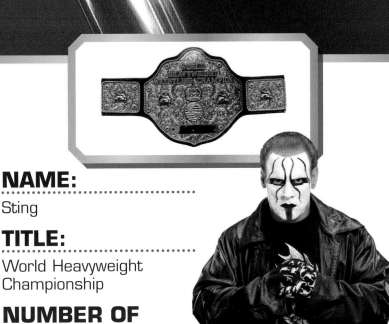

NAME:
Sting

TITLE:
World Heavyweight Championship

NUMBER OF TIMES WON:
Six

NAME:
Trish Stratus

TITLE:
Women's Championship

NUMBER OF TIMES WON:
Seven

Getting to *WrestleMania*

Every Superstar wants to compete at *WrestleMania*. It is WWE's biggest and most popular event.

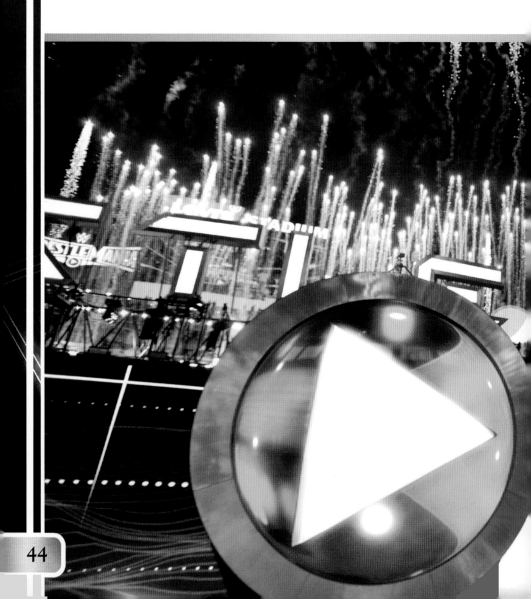

Millions of people watch every *WrestleMania* match. It is a chance to see the best Superstars perform.

Seth Rollins at *WrestleMania 31*

Becoming a champion

It is exciting to be a champion. The crowd always cheers for the winner. However, a champion must work hard to keep a championship.

Rivals will want to take the title for themselves. Just like John Cena, true champions never give up!

TAG TEAMS

Written by Steve Pantaleo

Meet the WWE Superstars

WWE Superstars are tough athletes. They compete in the ring to be the best.

Bayley and Sasha Banks

The Bar

Sometimes Superstars team up to form a tag team. They can team up with friends or even a member of their family.

What is a tag team?

Tag teams are groups of two or more Superstars. They take part in matches together.

One Superstar from each team battles at a time. When they want to swap places, teammates touch hands. This is called making a tag.

The Bar

Working together

Superstars often wear matching outfits to show they are a team.

The Usos

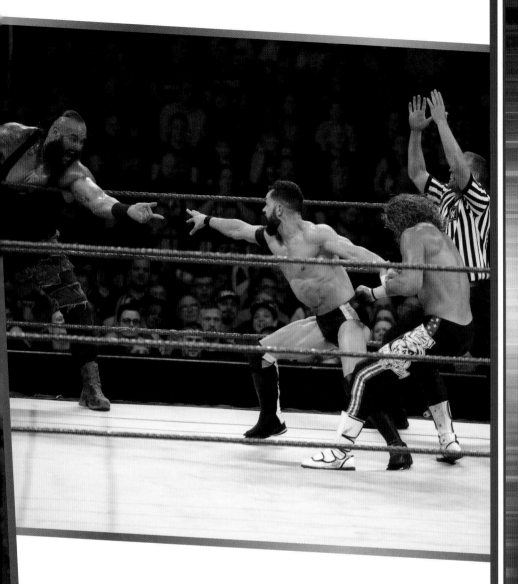

Switching places during a match stops Superstars from getting too tired. Here, Finn Bálor tags his teammate, Braun Strowman.

Making the tag

There are different ways to make a tag. Here are three.

Legal tag

A Superstar touches their teammate's hand to make a tag. This is a legal tag.

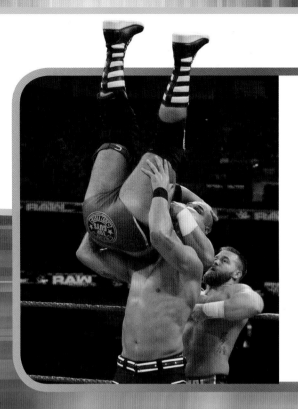

Blind tag

Sometimes a Superstar tags in without his opponent seeing. This is a blind tag.

Illegal tag

Superstars must tag from the corner of the ring. A tag from the middle of the ring is an illegal tag!

Twin power

The Bellas are identical twins. They have a trick to surprise their rivals. When one of them is tired, they secretly switch places. Their rivals don't realize they are fighting a fresh Superstar!

The Usos are also twins. They can each guess what the other will do next.

The New Day

Tag threes

The New Day has three members.
The Shield has three members,
too. They compete in three-on-
three matches.

The Shield bump fists before their matches. They are ready to compete as a team!

The Shield

Tag team titles

Tag teams fight for the *RAW* and *SmackDown* Tag Team Championships. The best team wins the title.

Dolph Ziggler

Titles are special belts. Winning teams wear their titles with pride! Dolph Ziggler and Drew McIntyre show off their titles.

Drew McIntyre

Match rules

WWE referees are always watching out for trouble. Breaking rules can get a tag team disqualified!

Only one Superstar from each team can wrestle at a time.

Once a tag is made, teammates have five seconds to switch places.

If a Superstar is pinned down, their partner can enter the ring. They have five seconds to help them.

The referee tells Jey Uso he has broken the rules!

The Usos

Face-off

Rival teams often trade insults before a match. Here, The New Day face off against their main rivals, The Usos.

The New Day

Tag team trouble

Even the best tag teams can fall out. Sometimes, teammates become jealous of each other.

Charlotte Flair and Becky Lynch used to be a team. They stopped getting along. Now, they are foes.

Champions

The Usos have won the
SmackDown Tag Team
Championship title three times.

The New Day were the
longest reigning champions.
They held the title for 483 days!
Champions need to watch
out. There will always be
another team ready to take
their title!

TEAM-UPS

Written by Steve Pantaleo

Unusual team-ups

Sometimes Superstars team up with their opposites, or even their enemies!

Former enemies

Sheamus and Cesaro used to be enemies. Now they are tag team champions!

Different styles

The Rock likes to be cool. Mankind is a rebel. Together, they make a winning team!

Hotheads

Daniel Bryan and Kane often argue with each other. They have won many matches.

Bending the rules

Sneaky teammates sometimes help from outside the ring. Here, Billie Kay pulls her teammate Peyton Royce away from Asuka's grasp.

Here, Drew McIntyre stops
Finn Bálor from climbing.
If the referee sees him, he
will be disqualified!

Hall of fame

Here are some of WWE's most famous teams. Some are from WWE history. Some are still fighting today!

New Age Outlaws
These rebels always caused chaos in the ring.

D-Generation X
Triple H and Shawn Michaels were not afraid to bend the rules!

The Hart Foundation

Bret "Hit Man" Hart and Jim "The Anvil" Neidhart were a super-strong team.

The Hardy Boyz

These brothers are hard to beat!

The Dudley Boyz

This tough team like to slam their enemies through tables!

Stables and factions

Sometimes a few Superstars join together. These groups are called stables and factions.

Finn Bálor formed the Bálor Club with his friends.

The Four Horsewomen inspire other female Superstars. They are strong and fearless!

SAnitY

SAnitY are a scary faction! They look spooky and they fight hard.

The members of SAnitY wear dark clothes. They paint their faces to scare their opponents.

The Riott Squad

Ruby Riott formed the Riott Squad with Sarah Logan and Liv Morgan. Their goal was to beat Charlotte Flair. Now, they want to beat everybody!

This fierce faction will do anything to win. They even attack their rivals backstage!

Survivor Series

At *Survivor Series*, teams from *RAW* and *SmackDown* battle. They battle until only one Superstar remains.

Team from *RAW*

Teams from *RAW* wear red. Teams from *SmackDown* wear blue. The winner gets to boast about being number one!

Team from *SmackDown*

Multi-team matches

A match between three teams is called a Triple Threat Match. A match with four teams is called a Fatal 4-Way.

Here, the Bludgeon Brothers take on The New Day and The Usos in a Triple Threat Match. Rowan leaps on Kofi Kingston and Jey Uso!

Quiz

1. What kind of tag is made without a Superstar's opponent seeing it?

2. True or false: The Bellas are identical twins.

3. How do the members of The Shield show they are ready to fight together?

4. Which risk-taking Superstar did The Rock team up with?

5. What are the special belts that Superstars win called?

6. How long do Superstars have to switch places after they have tagged each other?

7. What is the name of the stable formed by Finn Bálor?

8. Which faction wear face paint to scare its opponents?

9. Which Superstar formed the Riott Squad with Sarah Logan and Liv Morgan?

10. At *Survivor Series*, what color do teams from *RAW* wear?

Quiz

11. What is Sasha Banks's nickname?

12. Who plays the trombone?

13. What is Neville's signature move?

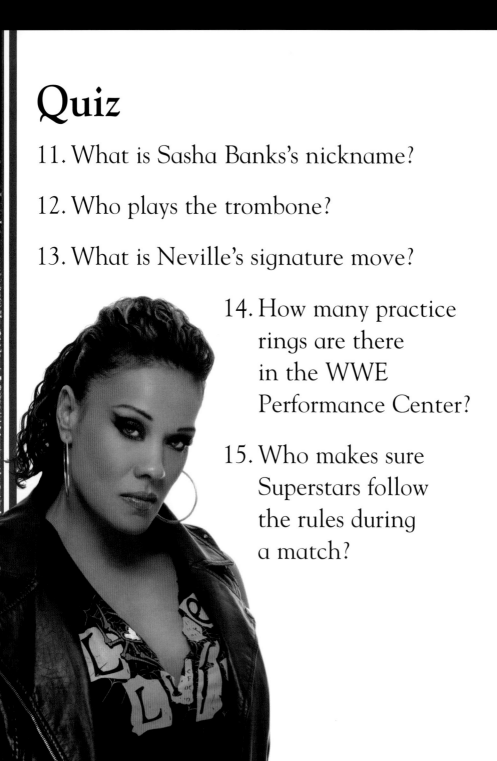

14. How many practice rings are there in the WWE Performance Center?

15. Who makes sure Superstars follow the rules during a match?

16. Which Superstar has a powerful Superman Punch move?

17. How high are the ladders in a Ladder Match?

18. How many times has Trish Stratus won the Women's Championship?

19. How often does Dolph Ziggler train to prepare for his matches?

20. Who is The Miz's manager?

Answers on page 94

Glossary

athlete
A person who is skilled at a sport.

audience
The people watching an event.

competitor
Someone who takes part in a contest.

disqualified
When someone loses a match because they have broken a rule.

foes
Enemies.

illegal
Against the rules.

opponent
Someone who competes against someone else in a contest.

personality
The qualities that make each person who they are.

signature move
A Superstar's best move in the ring.

tournament
A series of contests for a prize.

twins
Two siblings born to the same parents at the same time.

Answers to the quiz on page 90–93:
1. A blind tag 2. True 3. Bump fists 4. Mankind
5. Titles 6. Five seconds 7. The Bálor Club 8. SAnitY
9. Ruby Riott 10. Red 11. The Boss 12. Xavier Woods
13. Red Arrow 14. Seven 15. The referee 16. Roman Reigns
17. 20 ft. 18. Seven 19. Every day 20. Maryse

Index

Bayley 52

Becky Lynch 22, 70

Bret "Hit Man" Hart 25

Brock Lesnar 24

Cesaro 37

Charlotte Flair 35, 70, 86

Dean Ambrose 34

Dolph Ziggler 12–13

F5 24

Finn Bálor 57, 79, 82

John Cena 32–34, 46–47, 64–65

Ladder Match 16

managers 26–27

Maryse 27

Natalya 25

Neville 22–23

Randy Orton 25, 32–33

RAW 9

Red Arrow 22

Riott Squad 86

RKO 25

Roman Reigns 35

Ruby Riott 86

SAnitY 84–85

Sasha Banks 11, 52

Seth Rollins 10

Sharpshooter 25

Shawn Michaels 42

Sheamus 37

SmackDown Live 9

Steel Cage Match 17

Sting 43

tag teams 36–37

The Bálor Club 82

The Bar 53, 55

The Bellas 60

The Bludgeon Brothers 90–91

The Four Horsewomen 83

The Miz 27

The New Day 21, 62, 68–69, 73, 91

The Rock 18–19

The Shield 62–63

The Usos 36, 56, 61, 68–69, 72, 91

Trish Stratus 43

Wrestlemania 19, 44–45

Xavier Woods 21

A LEVEL FOR EVERY READER

This book is a part of an exciting four-level reading series to support children in developing the habit of reading widely for both pleasure and information. Each book is designed to develop a child's reading skills, fluency, grammar awareness, and comprehension in order to build confidence and enjoyment when reading.

Ready for a Level 2 (Beginning to Read) book

A child should:

- be able to recognize a bank of common words quickly and be able to blend sounds together to make some words.
- be familiar with using beginner letter sounds and context clues to figure out unfamiliar words.
- sometimes correct his/her reading if it doesn't look right or make sense.
- be aware of the need for a slight pause at commas and a longer one at periods.

A valuable and shared reading experience

For many children, reading requires much effort, but adult participation can make reading both fun and easier. Here are a few tips on how to use this book with a young reader:

Check out the contents together:

- read about the book on the back cover and talk about the contents page to help heighten interest and expectation.
- discuss new or difficult words.
- chat about labels, annotations, and pictures.

Support the reader:

- give the book to the young reader to turn the pages.
- where necessary, encourage longer words to be broken into syllables, sound out each one, and then flow the syllables together; ask him/her to reread the sentence to check the meaning.
- encourage the reader to vary her/his voice as she/he reads; demonstrate how to do this if helpful.

Talk at the end of each book, or after every few pages:

- ask questions about the text and the meaning of the words used—this helps develop comprehension skills.
- read the quiz at the end and encourage the reader to answer the questions, if necessary, by turning back to the relevant pages to find the answers.

Series consultant, Dr. Linda Gambrell, Distinguished Professor of Education at Clemson University, has served as President of the National Reading Conference, the College Reading Association, and the International Reading Association.